Floral
Mandala
Coloring Book
First name : ....
Last name : ....

Welcome to a world of
Floral Mandala. We have
created something special for
you. A beautiful coloring
book with floral mandala
collection. If you enjoy
coloring and want to escape
the stress of daily life and
relax, forgetting your troubles

copyright © 2020